POULTRY FARMING
A Beginners' Guide to Poultry Buiness

Grace A. Strong

Dedication

It is with joy that I dedicate this book to all beginners of poultry farming. I hope you find this business, profiting and adventurous.

Copyright

Table of Content

CHAPTER 1

Understanding Poultry Farming

Introduction

Poultry farming is a type farming that involves raising birds such as chickens, turkeys, ducks, and geese and getting from them, meat, eggs, and feathers for meeting the purpose of commercial and substantial agriculture. It is a type farming that is practiced all over the world in big and small scales.

We have two distinctive types of poultry farming: Intensive and Free-range. The practice of intensive farming involves growing a large number of birds in small areas often in cages and bans, with the provision of foods, water and other mineral needs. Free-range poultry farming on the other hand and as the name implies, permits the birds to roam about in search of natural foods and survival.

Poultry farming is speedily dominating the field of agriculture due to the continuously expanding high demand of its products. For instance, per capita consumption of eggs in the United States from 2000 to 2013 shows rather an increase. In 2000, consumption of eggs in the United States was estimated at 250% per person and 252 in 2001. It rose to 293.4 in 2019, 277.5 in 2021, and 288.6 in 2023. If by March, 2023, we have an estimate of 288.6, there is a tendency it might rise above the estimate recorded in 2019. The highest number of meat consumption in the United States was also recorded in 2018.

This brief analysis indicates the high demand of products from poultry farming, and hence, the need to venture and dominate the market system.

To ensure a high productivity and profit margin, you'll need to make available proper housing, feeding, and disease control as you take up the business of poultry farming. Proper housing involves, conducive ventilation, required lighting, adequate temperature and nesting boxes for egg-laying birds. Feeding has to do with providing for the birds a balanced diet that must include grains, protein, vitamins, and minerals. Disease control involves providing the birds a clean environment, providing vaccinations and other preventative measures, and taking prompt action whenever an illness is detected.

Benefits of Poultry Farming

Research has proven that chicken is one of the most consumed meat around the world today, with United States and India recording the highest estimates. Eggs and turkey meat are increasing daily on their consumption scale. When considering the merits and demerits of these products, there is the need to balance the profit demands from their sales and of course, the continuous food supply with the compassionate treatment of these birds throughout their lifetime. The following are some of the wide benefits one can derive from poultry farming:

1. **Poultry farming can involve a variety of other species**

   Though, chicken happens to be the major source of meat and eggs in the United States as over 5 billion of chickens are raised annually, you can also include other species such as turkey, geese, and ducks for a variety of unique products. Some farmers also exhaust the advantage of the chicken feathers by harvesting them as material products for stuffing.

   If you don't cherish the idea of slaughtering chickens like some of us don't, then you can spend more time on breeding and raising some layer hens and building your profit portfolio.

2. It Requires Less Capital for Startup

There is this notion of slacking during the start ups of businesses. You may have heard someone say, "I lack the capital to startup that business. I can afford it." With this notion, many businesses quench off before you know it. Agricultural business such as poultry farming requires less capital to start up in the first stage. Research from the University of Wisconsin shows that one can make a profit of $2.24 per bird (all things being equal) for an operation run with about 4,000 chickens sold. Poultry farming is a business one can even start up with a capital as low as $1000.

3. **Poultry farming can be very lucrative**

   If in the long run you decide to elevate your poultry business to a higher commercial level, then, you're sure of continuously receiving excellent profits from your startup capital if you're diligent. For instance, some of the poultry birds, like broilers take only few months to reach maturity. With this, you can seize that opportunity to raise 3-5 batches of the broilers in a year and supply to your relatives, friends and neighbours using your initial infrastructure.

4. **Poultry farming Requires Less Maintenance**

   Unlike other businesses, you don't need a much maintenance for your poultry business, mostly for one by a family operation. If you follow the required guidelines for hygiene disease control, then you'd be preventing the spread of diseases amongst your birds, thereby prolonging their lifespan. By so doing, you will also be protecting the spread of the disease to your family or household.

5. **It is a Source of Job Opportunity**
   Due to the limited job opportunities in the labour market, and because of poultry farming is a family business, you can teach your children the beauty of it and how to sustain and proliferate the business. Another beauty of this business, is, you can be running it while maintaining any other business, because its demands are of minimal attention.

CHAPTER 2

Preparing for Poultry Farming
Selecting a Suitable Site

Just every other business, selection of suitable location is one of the very important factors to consider when setting up a business. This also applies to setting up a poultry farm. Every business has its consumer and the tendency of succeeding in that business is linked to the nature of its location. Let's consider the following factors as necessities in selecting a suitable site for your poultry farming:

1. **Neigbourhood**

   One could be wondering what has neighbourhood got to do the selection of a suitable site for poultry business. It really does. Not every neighbour would be happy to have you setup such business around the hood. It could be because of the offensive odour that normally comes out from the facility, or the incessant trooping in to and from the farm by different calibers of people.

So, to maintain that good relationship with your neighbours and for the safety of your business, it is better to first call for a meeting with them to discuss your intention. If not accepted, it would be best to move it to another suitable location.

2. **Litter Management**

Litters are produced by the broilers on daily basis, hence, the need to manage it. It is estimated that approximately 300 tons of litter are produced yearly on a 50,000-capacity broiler farm. An analysis of the farm should be carried out to ascertain if it can hold the quantity and used as fertilizer or shifted offsite.

3. **Additional Buildings**

   Additional buildings such as ones for composting, litter storage, etc., should be considered as well. Because of this, a good land area to accommodate this necessity should also be considered. These additional buildings shouldn't be sited too far away from the main facility.

4. **Basic Amenities**

   The availability or closeness of basic amenities such as quality water, electricity should be of utmost consideration when choosing a location for a poultry farm.

5. **Closeness to Main Road**

   The location of a poultry facility should be sited far away from the main road. This is to avoid the unconducive noise from vehicles which could cause stress to birds, resulting to less or poor production.

6. **Exposure**: The poultry house should face south or east in most localities. A southern exposure allows more sunlight in the house than any of the other possible exposures. An eastern exposure is almost as good as a southern one. Birds prefer morning sunlight to that of the afternoon sunlight. The birds tend to be more

active in the morning and will spend more time in the sunlight.

Poultry Housing and Equipment

Good housing is necessary is a necessity to provide the birds with protection against adverse climatic effects such as direct sunlight, wind, rain, and even from predators such as cat, dogs, snakes, fox. Let's consider the following as housing requirements:

1. **Floor Space**

   The size of the house and the feet occupied by each hen is related. The smaller the house, the more the square feet occupied by each hen. Bigger pens allow more usable floor space per bird than small pens. Economically, it is good to keep the laying hens in small units of 15-25 birds.

2. **Ventilation**

Ventilation in the poultry house is necessary to provide them with adequate fresh air and eliminate moisture. Do you know the fowl is a small animal but has high metabolism? Its air requirement per unit of the body is much higher than other animals.

3. **Temperature**

For effective functioning of the hens' system, they need a moderate temperature of 50-70°F. They require a warmer temperature during the night when they're inactive than during the day. The introduction of insulation with straw pack serves to keep the poultry house warmer during the raining season and cold during the dry season.

Feed and Water Supply

Feeds that are of nutritional balance should be provided for your chicks. They can be bought from sellers or prepared in the farm. There three types produced by reliable companies for you to consider:

1. Starter feeds (with 8 weeks of age)
2. Grower feed (with 9 to 16 of age)
3. Layer feed (17 to 72 of age)

As a beginner of the business, it may interest you to know that you can actually prepare these feeds yourself in the farm. This is a simple way of managing your funds. The feed should be well-kept in a clean, dry and well-ventilated room. A deviance of any of these conditions, say, too much moisture, can lead to fungus or bacterial infections. Well-designed feeders should be used and these can be gotten from the market.

Space for feeding per bird and adequate quantity necessary for a bird, base on age and size is of utmost importance for the healthy growth of your birds. This is aided by frequently keeping records of feed consumption per bird to know when there is excess or low consumption, and consequently, the causes of these defects. Excess consumption may be due to attack by rats, inadequate temperature variation of sheds, etc. Low utilization may be due unrest of chicks as a result of disease infection, high temperature of sheds, and poor quality of feeds. These conditions must be looked after to ensure a proper yield.

Just as humans, the chicks cannot survive or thrive without clean water supply. So, the chicks should be provided with clean water regularly and ensure the proper use of water equipment. Enough drinking space per bird should also be considered. The water pot should always be kept clean and should be one not too big or deep to avoid the chicks falling into it. During summer, cool water should be provided and have a storage tank that is not exposed to direct sunlight.

CHAPTER THREE

Choosing the Right Breed for Your Farm
Factors to Consider

Now, that you've made up your mind to setup your poultry farm or you're all ready running your poultry business, there certain factors you should consider for effective yield. These factors have their direct and indirect capacity to impair or enhance your productivity. Let's look at some of these factors:

1. **Breeding Space**
   Have a good knowledge of the number of birds you have in your farm to provide them with enough

feeding space per bird. Some doesn't have the temperament to coexist in a smaller space with other chicks. These are active breeds are best raised in open lands as they are poor in handling confinement.

2. **Climate Condition**

When selecting your breeds of chicken for your poultry farming, consider the climate tolerance of your area. This is because the breeds show diverse reactions to climatic conditions. While some thrive in cold conditions, many find it difficult to exist in hotter climate conditions. It is important to note that some of these birds do well in both climatic conditions. To achieve a maximum yield, consider this factor when starting your poultry farm.

3. **Egg Production**

   If you're starting up a poultry farm for the purpose of egg production and sells, consider going for breeds that match that purpose. There are breeds of chicken that are suitable for meat as others are for eggs. A good breed can yield 125 to 175 eggs per year, per hen. Excellent production can exceed 230 to hit 300 per year, per hen. This shows the important of choosing the right breed for the right purpose.

4. **Meat Production**

   If you're considering raising chicken for purpose of meat production, you may like to go for breeds that suit that purpose. This is where maturation rate is considered. You'll have to go for breeds that take little time to mature in other to record multiple sales in a year and keep your customers in touch and needs satisfied.

These are the major factors/conditions to consider when choosing the right breeds for your poultry farm.

Popular Breeds for Eggs and Meat Production

Broilers are specie of chicken raised specifically for their product, meat. They're reared and sold when matured in large numbers and at the same time to maintain biosecurity. They are typically white in colour and are bred for optimal health and size to meet the consumer needs of the product.

There are different breeds of chicken that have been reared for different purposes. These can be summarized into 3, viz: egg laying, meat production and dual-purpose.

1. The Cornish Breed

   The meat producing breed are very efficient at generating approximately one pound of weight for every two pounds of feed they consume. The Cornish breed is a popular meat-producing breed. They're rapid in their growth and weigh about five pounds in eight weeks. Today, they're most popular amongst commercial producers because of their rapid growth and gain of weight in a short span of time than other species.

2. Bresse

Bresse is another breed with efficient meat production and very popular in the market because of its sweet taste. This make them very expensive, but they're it. The Bresse thrives well in flock and love to roam about with other chickens. They weigh 6-7 pounds and ready for harvest between 16-20 weeks.

3. Buckeyes

These are the breeds of chicken that can strongly withstand cold climate and have the capacity to resist many disease infections, making them popular for backyard farmers. The bukeyes is basically a dual-purpose breed, producing about 200 eggs per year and often takes a longer time to mature.

They weigh 6-9 pounds and are ready for harvest between 16-21 weeks.

4. Dorkings

The dorking has a very attracting body and docile. They're unaggressive and do well when placed amongst aggressive species because they lack the defense capacity. They don't do well in cold climate conditions. They rather thrive in warmer condition. They produce about 140 eggs in a year. Not quite good, because they're known more for their large meat production. They weigh 7-9 pounds and are harvested within 16 weeks.

5. The Freedom Ranger

The freedom ranger is a quiet breed that loves quiet environment. Though, it has slow maturity rate, its meat is of high quality and flavored. Because of its size, it does not produce much quantity of meat like other breeds. It is unaggressive and very friendly with people. It prefers to run around freely and hunts for bugs and grasses. They weigh 5-6 pounds and are harvested in 16 weeks.

These are some of the popular breeds of chicken known for their eggs and bountiful meat production. A good knowledge of these breeds is pertinent when starting and building your poultry business.

www.ingramcontent.com/pod-product-compliance
Lightning Source LLC
Chambersburg PA
CBHW071147220526
45467CB00015B/2066